It's Time
to Live

IT'S TIME TO LIVE

by Ronald C. Starenko

CONCORDIA PUBLISHING HOUSE
St. Louis   London

Concordia Publishing House, St. Louis, Missouri
Concordia Publishing House Ltd., London, E. C. 1
© 1969 Concordia Publishing House
Library of Congress Catalog Card No. 69 – 18865

MANUFACTURED IN THE UNITED STATES OF AMERICA

CONTENTS

5

INTRODUCTION

Time is a problem for us. Sometimes we have too much to do and too little time in which to do it; sometimes we have too much time and too little to do with it. Our problem with time is really a frustration with life.

Thinkers of every age have expressed frustration with time and life. The author of Ecclesiastes, for example, is troubled because man cannot change the rhythm of time. A power directs it over which he has no control. He complains that everything is vanity: "I have seen everything that is done under the sun; and behold, all is vanity and a striving after wind." He implies that all time is meaningless and senseless.

We suffer from a similar anxiety. We say that "time marches on," but we are not sure if we should be happy or sad, for time can be a friend or an enemy. We say that "time heals," but if that is true, we must also say that time wounds. We look at our clocks and see that time seems to go in a circular motion. This creates an illusion, as if time were always repeating itself, as if we would always have an opportunity to do tomorrow what we should have done today. But the dawn of one day cannot by itself remove the darkness of the one before.

The ancient Greeks believed they had an answer to this problem. They thought that time essentially had no meaning, that the ideal was timelessness. They set their minds on the world that is apart from or comes after this one, on the eternal. According to their view, time is something to be tolerated, endured.

A trace of this has crept into Christian thinking. Some Christians believe time must give way to timelessness, that the temporal must be replaced by the eternal before there can be any meaning in life and in time.

The Bible presents a different approach to time. Against the somewhat bleak view expressed by the Preacher which reflects man's problem, the Scriptures also describe God's penetration into time. He is pictured not only as One who stands above it all but also as One who is involved in it all.

God created time for a blessing to mankind, for our use and enjoyment. We dare not despise, fear, or kill time.

We are not called to live according to wristwatch time but according to alarm-clock time. In the New Testament the present moment is always the important moment. We are not called to live for some other time. In Paul's words, "Behold, now is the acceptable time; behold, now is the day of salvation" (2 Corinthians 6:2). We cannot live in the past; we cannot live in the future. We cannot undo the past; we cannot determine the future. We live now or not at all!

God has acted within time. He has made Himself part of our days and years and experiences. When Christ entered the world, God gave meaning to our time. He joined us in the Incarnation. In the cross He took care of the past; in the Resurrection the future. We are at all times in the hands of the living, loving God, for whom there is also a time for everything, a time for us.

That means it is time to live. It is no longer necessary to mark time, to escape the past or future, to worry about what happened or what may happen. There is no need to avoid the present by trying to recapture the "good old days" or by dreaming of some Shangri-la. God is present with us.

It's time to live, even when we are troubled by apparent worthlessness and meaninglessness in life, tortured by failure and fear, or tormented by suffering and death.

*1

WHEN IT DOESN'T SEEM WORTH IT

One day in a hospital I visited a woman who had attempted suicide by taking an overdose of pep pills. She was the mother of six children. Though divorced, she had several suitors. She received weekly payments for child support, enough to spend on a vacation in Florida shortly before her suicide attempt. And she was only 36 years old. Yet she insisted, "I have nothing to live for!"

One might think she had a lot to live for—

money, children, lovers. We might conclude that she must have been "out of her head" to try to take her own life. Perhaps. But for the moment let us ask ourselves what we have to live for.

What keeps us going? Our children? They will grow up before we know it. Our youth? It passes away. Our income? It can change overnight. We may not have thought of swallowing pills or putting a gun to our heads or jumping from a bridge. But what if we lost everything we now have and enjoy? Would we still feel we have something to live for?

Even the great apostle Paul wrestled with this problem. Sitting in a prison cell awaiting trial, he assessed his life and wondered whether it was worth living. He concluded that Christ would be honored in his body whether by life or by death. Then he made the amazing statement: "To me to live is Christ, and to die is gain." (Philippians 1:21)

In his book *The Adventure of Living,* Paul Tournier writes about the dissatisfied, for those who become increasingly aware of something missing in their lives. "Woe betide those," he says, "who no longer feel thrilled at anything, who have stopped looking for adventure." He cites typical examples of people who fail to fulfill themselves, who never discover a coordinating center to their lives, who are like willows in the wind. The clock watcher works day after day at a job that holds no interest for him, because he lacks the adventurous drive to find and develop the special talent given to every human being. Some lose themselves in popular films, novels, and TV shows sooner than investigate their own creative abilities. Parents identify themselves with their children in the pathetic hope of realizing the dream they themselves missed. A man maintains a mistress for excitement because he finds his marriage deadly dull, not troubling to make the marriage itself exciting. The hypochondriac makes illness a desperate search for adventure. All are people who can never seem to find themselves, who never find the real adventure of living, because they try to find value in substitutes, in money, sex, or political power. All are trying to find a new center.

Paul shows that he found a new center in these words: "To me to live is Christ." He discovered that living is not mere existing, moving from instinct to instinct, using up something as long as one has it. Life for him was not a thing at all; it was a person — Jesus Christ.

We cannot live in and of ourselves; we cannot really live by and for ourselves. Life is not surviving; it is sharing. And we have a life to share, a life that was lived for others, a life that knew the cross but also experienced the resurrection. Christ's life has become our life.

Christ affirmed our worth, because He died for us. His Word remains His witness to us that we can live, because His life has become our very own. In Christ we have a new center, a new self.

When we know Christ, we say no to our false substitute centers and yes to Him. Nothing else can fulfill our lives — not pleasure, power, possessions, position, plans, potential; for none of these live for us, none have the power to give us life, none can make us new. Only Jesus Christ, who brings divine love and forgiveness into the world, can be our life, for only He has lived and died for us.

It's time to live when it doesn't seem worth it, because our worthless life has been restored. To say, "To me to live is Christ," is to believe that we are alive, that the whole adventure of life has a new meaning. The life we live is the life of God, given and guaranteed through Jesus Christ.

But Paul says more. He also writes to his readers at Philippi: "To die is gain." This is the affirmation of a man who faces death and yet does not believe he is being cheated. He did not live simply as an attempt to avoid death, for the life he lived was already the new life beyond death. For St. Paul death was no longer a pivotal, a focal point of life. He did not worship death as if it had the power to take from him the life he had received from Christ. In other words, death for him was not the great failure. If for him to live was Christ, death would mean more of Christ, a step closer to Christ. The life he lived now was not only worth living — it was also worth dying for!

That is not an easy affirmation for us to make.

People everywhere live in the fear of death. Even if they have succeeded in blocking from their consciousness that there is an end of the road marked by a grave, underneath they are driven to use their life as if its only purpose were to avoid death as long as possible.

While I was on training duty one summer with the U. S. Marines in California, a young pfc came into my office and said, "Chaplain, I'm worried; I don't want to be 'zapped' when I go to Vietnam." A normal concern, we would agree, and yet at that moment he feared death as though it were a god. To clutch at life or cast it away is the reaction of one who believes fanatically in death.

Sometimes we delude ourselves into thinking that enjoying "the full life" to the hilt can remove the sting of death. Yet beneath the surface of our consciousness stirs the suspicion that something threatens to destroy our happiness and upset our plans. It is our fear of death. Why is it that we are so afraid of being poor or sick or unemployed? We sense the power of death. To die

18

seems to be loss and not gain: to die is to fall victim to the inevitable, the unavoidable. And to live with such fear is not to live at all. It is a desperate captivity that results from clinging compulsively to life or frivolously casting it away.

From this fate we have been delivered. To die is gain not simply because we escape into another world but because the power of death in this world has already been broken. The life we live in Jesus Christ is a new life beyond death. To have Christ's life is to have also His power over death. As William Stringfellow has written: "There is no pain or privation, no humiliation or disaster, no distress or hunger, no striving or temptation, no sickness or suffering or poverty, which God has not known and borne for men in Jesus Christ. He has borne death itself on behalf of men, and in that event He has broken its power once and for all." (*My People Is the Enemy,* p. 32)

We identify with Christ's power over death in Holy Baptism. We celebrate His resurrection victory in the Lord's Supper. We know the victory in the hearing of the Gospel. The Good News is that we are beyond death now. It does not mean that we never know sin and death; it means rather that sin and death can no longer rob us of the life and worth we have in Jesus Christ.

When life doesn't seem worth it, we look at the living Christ, and we know it's time to live.

2

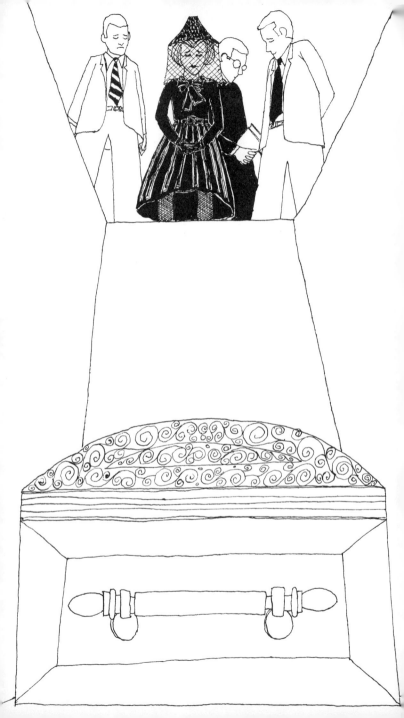

* *2*

WHEN YOU CAN'T GO ON

The chief character in Arthur Miller's play *Death of a Salesman* is Willy Loman, a man obsessed with the desire to succeed. Frustrated, he returned home after his sales trips to say, "I'm tired to the death." Eventually he sensed his failure as he echoed these words: "They don't need me in New York."

It then became his ambition to see success in his sons. He told them to go out and "lick the world," but they became a disappointment to him. When the world began to close in on him, he said at one point, "Work a lifetime to pay off a house. You finally own it, and there's nobody to live in it." One of his sons found out about his affair with another woman. Finally in his despair he sped off in his car to die in a suicidal crash.

At the funeral one of the sons said, "He had the wrong dreams. . . . He never knew who he was." His wife, staring into his grave, moaned: "Forgive me, dear, I can't cry. I don't know what it is, but I can't cry. I don't understand it. Why did you ever do that? Help me, Willy, I can't cry. It seems to me that you're just on another trip. I keep expecting you. Willy, dear, I can't cry. Why did you do it? I search and search and I search, and I can't understand it, Willy. I made the last payment on the house today. Today, dear. And there'll be nobody home. We're free and clear. We're free. We're free." And so a dramatic and tragic portrayal of frustration, failure, fear, and finality comes to a close with a despairing cry: "We're free and clear."

We too are caught up in the world of Willy Loman. The details are different, but our experience is marked by frustration, failure, fear, and finality. Ours is a world of wrong dreams too.

But this is the very world into which God came to redeem through Jesus Christ. St. Paul saw this world transformed. In his second letter to the Christians at Corinth he writes: "Therefore, if anyone is in Christ, he is a new creation; the old has passed away; behold, the new has come." (2 Corinthians 5:17)

Willy Loman did not know that the former things had passed away. He lived and died by those things that have no power to destroy death, to give life. He did not live with the reality of a living Christ who says, "Behold, I make all things new." (Revelation 21:5)

The life of Willy Loman gives us some insight into the meaning of sin. We usually think of sin in terms of morality, of being right or wrong, good or bad. Sin has a deeper meaning. The fall of man was not primarily a fall *into* weakness or materialism or sensuality; it was a fall *from* something, a breaking loose from God, an attempt to find life and its meaning in ourselves and in our accomplishments. In Willy Loman we see that the fall of man is an attempt to create life ourselves, to exist without a Creator and a Restorer of life. Sin, then, is living in the old order, a level of existence in which we can only pretend to be alive.

In our sober and more honest moments, however, we know that we are the victims of futility. Even Willy Loman knew that much. The only way out, he thought, was to end it all. Willy Loman had a dream, but he had no hope. He longed for release, but he had no victory to hang on to.

Can we recognize the same longing in our own lives? The old order still bothers us. Frustration takes its toll. We come home and say, "I feel like the devil," or "I feel like hell," or, "Boy, am I dead!" Figurative expressions perhaps, but they show that our existence is being drained of its life. We may have an unconscious desire to be released from the confines of this world with its limited time and energy. We get tired out. And sometimes we feel certain we can't go on.

Our exhaustion is more than physical or mental. We drag the weight of the past into every day of life. The worries of yesterday are still with us today. We live with a sense of failure, with the burden of regrets. We wish things could be different, that we might have a chance to take back what we said, to reverse a decision.

Willy Loman couldn't turn the clock back. He was not able to cope with the reality of his declining ability, his expendability, his being shoved right out of the company. The rat race of spending his energies on keeping a job, buying a home, rearing a family added up to nothing. He was a failure; success was only an illusion.

At such a point of self-examination panic sets in. We become scared, even if we do not show it on the outside. We sense that life is narrowing down. Things that once seemed important start slipping away. Fear overwhelms and torments us. Willy Loman tried to escape from his fear into a relationship with another woman. Other escapes include alcohol, pleasure seeking, spending and buying. We may think these can give us the courage to go on. But fear cannot be removed by escape techniques. It will remain to haunt us and perhaps lead us to consider suicide.

The thought of suicide is much more common today than we think. We may not feel that we exhibit a suicidal tendency; we are nevertheless hungry and thirsty people. We long to be released from the old order, the former things. We want to be free. We want to live.

It is time to live even when we are sure we can't go on. But we cannot do it by our own power. When we try to make life ourselves, we only make death. By trying to shape our own destiny we fall victim to the powers of the old order.

Into our world God came in Jesus Christ to declare that His dwelling is with men. He makes them His people. He destroys the power of death. God Himself interrupts the fatal sequence of frustration, fear, failure, and finality. He reveals through Jesus Christ that the old has gone to the cross with Christ in death. A new creation has broken in on this existence. "He who did not spare His own Son but gave Him up for us all, will He not also give us

all things with Him?" (Romans 8:32). All things!
In everything we are more than conquerors!

The risen Christ brings a goodness and a new
life to us. We no longer look to the past for
something to make our lives significant. We do
not depend on the present moment. Our claim
to life is in the new life in Christ. He forgives
our past. He stills our fears. He guarantees eternal
life. It is time to live, for in the risen Christ God
has revealed our final destiny.

The new life has begun, but we are not yet
in heaven. The old order and the new creation
stand side by side. We have not yet risen from
the grave. We still live in this present world. Our
new life is still largely hidden. But we continue
on in Christ, in the confidence of His resurrection,
in the certainty that we shall rise with Him.

We go through the country of the enemy, the
old order, announcing that it has been defeated,
celebrating the victory of Christ, crying out over
our own graves, not in despair but in hope, "We're
free and clear!"

It is time to live when you're sure you can't
go on!

*3

* 3

WHEN YOU MUST PRETEND TO BE HAPPY

A teen-ager put it this way:

> No matter what may fall my way,
> Life keeps on going day by day.
> By pretending to be happy and gay
> I shall live out my stay.

She speaks for many of us these days who want to be and try to be happy. We try to make joy happen. But the more we try to squeeze joy out of life, the less we have, and our anxiety increases.

Still we try to make it happen. We set our hearts on things, good things like family, success, beauty. Yet we see these things slip away. The result is a nagging anxiety that results either from failing to achieve what we attempt or from fearing the loss of what we have created. In either case we miss joy, and what remains is a sham and a fraud. We end up pretending.

The apostle Paul once urged his friends in Philippi to rejoice. At first glance it would seem that he was asking them to pretend to rejoice, for in his own case there was every reason in the world not to be joyful. He was behind bars. He had not planned to end up in a death cell. Things didn't seem to work out for him. How could he talk about rejoicing?

Our plans may be changed too. We discover that we feel trapped. We may say, "I was born at the wrong time, went to the wrong schools, got into the wrong job, married the wrong woman."

There is more. How do you get joy when you can no longer do your job? Paul was a preacher of the Gospel. Wherever he went, it was a challenge, an adventure, a joy to preach. And nobody could match his persuasiveness in preaching. But what can you do in a prison cell?

How many times we have been prevented from doing what we wanted to do! We all have egos that push us into activity. We can't seem to let up even for a minute, so anxious are we in pursuit of a goal we have set for ourselves. And how easily something can put us on the shelf!

St. Paul was not just on the shelf; he was staring into the grave. On many occasions prior to his imprisonment in Philippi he had escaped dangers of every kind. But now he had reached the end of the road, and he was afraid.

Nobody really counts on dying, and we protest it every inch of the way. Death is the ultimate tyranny, scratching what we are and what we have done. If joy is found in what we have become and what we have accomplished, then death is the greatest of our enemies. Faced with that, who can with calm and composure write off death as "one

35

of those things"? Who can philosophize about having had a "full life" and accept death without a whine or a whimper?

We can spin out our cases in defense of despair, for it would appear that we are fighting a losing battle if joy is something up for grabs. Inevitably we learn that we do not always get what we want; and when we do get what we want, we do not always get out of it what we hoped we would.

With backs to the wall we meet an inescapable fact: Joy is hard to find and easy to lose. Or could it be that what we think is joy is but a delusion? When St. Paul says, "Rejoice," he is referring to something that does not come by human achievement. Joy we cannot shape or create. What we keep running after in order to be happy and gay is really an idol, for our circumstances, our helplessness, our death convince us that the best we can do is to pretend.

The sooner we learn that the better. You think Paul had reason to despair — that you have reason to despair — in view of the crazy circumstances of life? Well, it wasn't circumstances that gave Paul joy to begin with, and circumstances were not going to take it from him. You think he had reason to throw in the towel and stare into space because his active life suddenly came to a dead stop? Should you think life is over when you get gray and begin to feel your age? Well, Paul didn't count on youth and beauty and productivity to bring him joy; so the loss of these things would not deprive him of joy. You think he might have had reason to believe his life was a waste, an unsuccessful venture, because death was knocking at the door? Should you lie down and die because you're going to die anyhow someday? Well, to go on living was not for Paul a reason for joy; and even death would not cheat him out of joy.

How could it? Joy is a gift. Paul didn't make it happen; it happened to him. He didn't possess it; it possessed him. Those who say the apostle was made of exceptional stuff, the kind you don't find today, are only fooling themselves. Paul didn't make himself joyful. And joy has nothing to do with being lucky or with being born under the right star. Joy is God's gift.

God's love, you see, took the shape of a real flesh-and-blood man who gave Himself, spent Himself to redeem and heal people. Joy happened in Jesus Christ, in Him whose light men tried to snuff out, whose life they tried to destroy, whom God raised from death to be life and light even for those who do not want it. So brightly and so strongly should it beam and bore in upon them that they would want it and take it to themselves and be changed by it. Joy comes as the Gospel, the Good News of God's love in Christ, transcends the circumstances of our life and gives a meaning to it that no man can give or take away. Joy is a gift and act of God.

So joy is here. Paul wrote: "Rejoice in the Lord always; again I will say, Rejoice. . . . The Lord is at hand. Have no anxiety about anything. . . . And the peace of God, which passes all understanding, will keep your hearts and your minds in Christ Jesus." (Philippians 4:4-7)

The miracle has already happened. The Lord is here, at hand, reaching out to us through the Holy Spirit to grasp us. Joy is ours. We don't have to imagine it or fashion it or scramble for it or pretend to have it. We don't have to try to straighten out all the circumstances in our lives to find it. Joy is ours in Christ Jesus. We don't have to achieve a certain goal in life or reach a certain status in society to be happy. Joy and peace is ours in Jesus Christ, and therefore we can take risks and can accept both failure and success for the sake of joy. We don't have to run from death any more than we must run to it, because we have life, God's life, eternal in Jesus Christ, a joy without end.

That same teen-ager who introduced this chapter continues:

> O God, hear my cry
> Or let me die!
>
>> No longer can I be
>> Just a drop in the sea;
>> I have a feeling, a longing,
>> Which comes from not belonging.
>> In order to survive
>> I have to feel alive.
>> It has been shown to me
>> That through Your agony and strife

And by Your suffering on a tree
I have been given Life.
Now I want to go out
And really sing and shout
About the Life I've found
Living within Your bounds.
To do Your will
Is truly the way to fill
My empty life of the past
With a future that will last.

O God, You answered my cry.
I no longer wish to die!

When you must pretend to be happy, it's time
to live. For joy has come into the world!

* *4*

* *4*

WHEN YOU CAN'T STAND THE PAIN

A man comes to his pastor for help. It is obvious that he is terribly troubled. He is suffering from a sense of guilt, grieving because he had been unfaithful to his wife. He knows his guilt and needs forgiveness. That man is on the road to healing. In his case, grief had a constructive value. It led to repentance and new life.

A woman comes to ventilate what she considers to be her problem. She is anxious, suspicious of

43

others, afraid — a nervous wreck. She is suffering too. She says that nobody loves her, that her husband is an impatient man, that her children won't behave, that there are financial problems, and she gets headaches. She is looking for sympathy, for someone to join her against those who seem so threatening, for someone who will do something about that husband of hers and those children. She sorrows, but she does not want to change; she wants others to change. Such grief is destructive because it is an evasive tactic, a refusal to see that the problem is with herself.

We may not find ourselves in such desperate predicaments, but this does not mean we are without grief. Every person carries in his heart some hurt, some trouble, some problem, some anxiety. The question is not: Do we have grief? Nor: Should we have grief? Rather: Is our grief worldly or godly? Is it negative or positive, destructive or constructive?

That the purpose of life is to avoid all pain, or that the Christian faith guarantees the absence of grief, is an illusion. It is unrealistic to suppose that life can become "uninterrupted radiant happiness." Sooner or later people awaken to the sober realities of life.

We all know people who become resentful toward God when their hopes in life have been dashed. People who think life has played them a cruel trick, who feel they have been deprived of something they deserve, have not learned to cope with life or with themselves. They are full of regrets. They are always thinking about how things might have been, how they should be, how they must be. When their sorrow becomes unbearable, they look for a tranquilizer.

Some people approach the Christian Gospel in the same manner. They want something to soothe their pain. They don't want forgiveness of sins; they just don't want to feel guilty about their sins. They don't want to be resurrected to a new life; they just don't want to be reminded about death. They don't want any part in the experience of repentance; they prefer a message that reinforces their own attitudes and ambitions.

This is illustrated in a letter written by a pastor: "One of our members is a bit disturbed. He is now missing church every other Sunday or so, because of my preaching. He feels that I'm talking to the people who aren't there, to the sinners instead of the Christians. My sermons depress him, he says, or to quote him directly: 'I'm a sinner, I know that; everyone is, but I don't like to be reminded of it all the time. Church should make me feel good!' Then yesterday I get the comment from one of the ladies in the congregation who had had some real problems with herself: 'I've never heard myself described so well as the sermons do, and I've never known how much Jesus Christ could mean to me.'"

The implication of all this is quite clear: The Word that leads a person along the path to healing involves pain. Those who will not bear it live only with "worldly grief."

Such sorrow that blocks healing is of two kinds: self-pity and self-defensiveness.

People who feel sorry for themselves experience grief, but it is destructive. Such people complain how badly things are going for them, how unjustly they are being treated. They never take a hard look at themselves. They are unwilling to go through the pain of self-honesty. Consequently they are never really open to healing and are unreceptive to divine forgiveness. Their grief does not lead to repentance and renewal. It is a worldly grief, because it is a selfish grief.

The self-defensive person is usually aggressive and hostile toward others. He attacks other people because he is convinced that the world's troubles and his own personal problems are caused by others. A person with a self-defensive attitude can destroy marriage by relentlessly accusing the other person or by demanding that he change.

Such grief does not flow from God. Such stubborn, selfish reactions block the free movement of confession and forgiveness. Such is the worldly grief that produces death.

The other pain in life is worked by God and becomes a positive healing power in our lives. Suffering can be helpful. We can experience a purpose and a meaning in our sorrows when we understand them as part of the healing process.

Our grief becomes a godly grief when we

consider the sorrows of God. The suffering of Christ was caused by our selfishness, by our inhumanity to others, our hostility toward God, our determination to remain what we are. That is the sin that Christ endured in His death. That is the sin that God exposes and forgives. In the grief of Jesus Christ God has turned us to Himself. Through the suffering of our Lord God gives us promise and hope. This makes our grief something positive. In His grief we discover it's time to live when we are certain we can't stand the pain.

Paul once took the Corinthians to task for their moral and spiritual apathy. And they reacted to his criticism. They grieved. But he recognized their inner suffering as something that had a positive effect. This is what he wrote in response: "As it is, I rejoice, not because you were grieved into repenting; for you felt a godly grief, so that you suffered no loss through us. For godly grief produces a repentance that leads to salvation and brings no regret, but worldly grief produces death." (2 Corinthians 7:9-10)

* 5

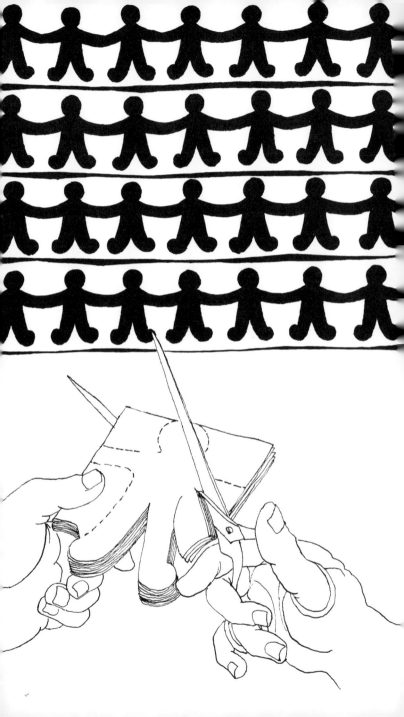

* 5

WHEN LIFE SEEMS EMPTY

During World War II French doctors coined a name for a disease that appeared in prison camps. They called it "barbed-wire sickness." One of its symptoms was an appalling sense of the futility of life. Cut off from the rest of the world, many prisoners could not function. Their lives had lost all significance and meaning.

People suffer "barbed-wire sickness" today. But the problem is not simply that we have trouble finding any good in the bad things; what we call the good often leaves us with a feeling of emptiness. Death fills us with fear, but so does the thought of living. We find very little good in anything when we cannot see every experience and event of life as part of God's gracious design.

We need some glimpse of a plan, a word from God that in everything He is working for our good, that the destiny He has provided for us makes our living now triumphant and significant.

A young woman of twenty thought she was getting old. She was panicky about it, almost desperate, because she had no immediate prospects for marriage. She was ready to marry, if she had the chance, just to be married. She was not challenged by her work, though it could have been a real form of service. Having very few lasting values in life, she was stumbling along without any compelling goals. Lacking a sense of identity as a child of God, she had no understanding of His purposes for her life.

This young woman is one of many who live without a future. Unable to see beyond the everyday experiences of pain and pleasure, they are not open to the power and plan of God in their lives. When we try desperately to obtain possessions, position, and power, we are really trying to secure ourselves against the future. When we try to forge our own future, we become afraid that we will never achieve the success or happiness we want.

A future based on our own strivings never arrives. We may bank on something great happening just around the next corner, next year, when the house is paid off, when the children grow up, when we can have our own business, when we can retire. Such a future is no future, for we have excluded God and sealed ourselves in "barbed-wire sickness."

Yet God has a goal for our lives. He has already revealed the future to us in the good news of the Gospel. Our destiny has been established. Our lives have received eternal significance through God's plan disclosed in Jesus Christ, in the life and victory He attained, in the forgiveness and love He brought to the world.

For the needs of this life we must still make

financial and retirement plans, but God's purposes for us do not depend on the completion of our plans. God has destined us to be conformed to the image of His Son, to live through suffering and death with the assurance of everlasting life with Him. Because of Christ we can say with Paul "that in everything God works for good with those who love Him, who are called according to His purpose." (Romans 8:28)

Everything? A divorce, a heart attack, death by cancer, a crippled or handicapped child? These are things for good?

Never! we are tempted to say. How can evil and trouble be termed good? If our logic excludes the power and plan of God, we live as fatalists. "That's the way the ball bounces," we say, or, "It just wasn't in the cards."

In the face of this "everything," God has given us a look into His plan through Jesus Christ. On the surface much of our Lord's life appeared to be disastrous and frustrating, yet God turned everything for our good, because through Him He triumphed over evil and death. No evil frustrated

God's purposes in His Son, and nothing that happens in our lives will prevent Him from saving us and bringing us to glory.

God's great purpose gives us certainty and confidence. Nothing in our lives happens by chance. It was not by chance that Christ was born; it was not by chance that you were born. It was not by chance that Christ overcame every power hostile to man; and it will not be by chance that we shall overcome by faith in Him. We are caught up now in God's plan.

In Romans 8 Paul writes as one caught up in the power of the Gospel amid life's struggles. Finding himself on the side of Christ, Paul is moved to praise God for the victory of Christ and the revelation of His will. His awareness that God had chosen him in Christ moves him to greater faith in God's provident grace. Paul has a certain audacity of faith that in God he has a destiny in spite of everything.

Helmut Thielicke writes: "It is the adoration of a man who is at the end of all his potentialities, who is conscious only of the disaster to which his guilt has doomed him, and now is snatched away from all this by the strange initiative of God and led by the Father's hand into the cheerful light of home." (*Man in God's World,* p. 206)

Life is not empty after all. The problems of today and tomorrow do not abort God's design for us. We do not live in a barbed-wire enclosure but in the expanse of God's gracious plan.

Life is like looking at a stained-glass window. From the outside it appears dark and dirty. From the inside we see the light shine through the dirt and grime in colorful splendor. When we stand within the good news of the Gospel, we see the light of His grace shine through to reveal the beauty of His gracious plan. We can say that "in everything God works for good with those who love Him, who are called according to His purpose."

It's time to live when life seems empty.

*6

* 6

WHEN YOU FEEL DEFEATED

Loren Eiseley in his book *The Firmament of Time* views with considerable horror the vanishing order of nature under the thundering engine of modern technology. He sees a vast open hole in nature, a vast black whirlpool spinning faster and faster, something frightening, something demonic.

   If it is true that we are moving toward a whirlpool and that technology serves only to give us a glimpse of the demise of our universe, the

59

psalmist was right when he wrote that we are "accounted as sheep for the slaughter." (Psalm 44:22)

What is there to prevent such a fate? We can say it will never happen to us. We can put the blanket over our heads and pretend we aren't in the 20th century. But we cannot escape the defeat we feel inside.

We can learn from a man who knew how to answer back when things were giving way around him. The apostle Paul knew everything about life that's ugly and threatening — tribulation, distress, persecution, famine, nakedness, peril, and sword — everything that says we are vulnerable. But in the face of everything that contradicts life, Paul points to God's Christ as our rebuttal, to Him who died, yes, who was raised from the dead.

Like a madman he says, "No, in all these things we are more than conquerors through Him who loved us" (Romans 8:37). God is not against us; He is still for us.

This does not mean there will never be anything around to defeat us. But it does mean that we can always count on God to deliver us. God makes no promise that life will become uncomplicated for those who believe. People yearn for some private peace of mind or the preservation of our Western civilization. People want to hang on to the luxury of a world surrounded by two cars, a six-pack, and an idiot box. To have all that, they will hurry and scurry about hysterically looking for a remedy. A woman, suffering deep-seated emotional problems that went back to rejection by her parents, informed me that she had been seeing a therapist for about two years and had acquired some insights. She told me, "After 27 years I'm just beginning to realize that there is no panacea for problems, no Cinderella-type existence where everything sooner or later goes away like a bad dream."

The love of God we know in Christ is not so much an answer for the problems of living as it is the solution for the problem of life. There is a difference. The problems of living are inescapable. St. Paul found that to be true. There was no way in the world he could get around tribu-

61

lation, distress, persecution, famine, nakedness, peril, or sword. There is no way we can prevent disappointment, loneliness, and frustration. We may set up our little gods and develop other infantile ways of escaping and hiding from these things, but sooner or later they will have conquered us. The problem of life is being able to cope with these things. The Gospel prepares us to get through and not merely get out.

The call of God is to trust in His love in the face of all these things, to believe His victory in the face of defeat. The challenge of every believer is to cling to the incredible love of the God who lets us get killed all the day long as sheep to be slaughtered, who lets His own Son be killed as the Lamb to be slaughtered.

The Gospel does not put an end to troubles, but it does put an end to our strivings to escape defeat. Look what it meant to St. Paul. He was not a stoic who faced life by gritting his teeth. He wasn't a hedonist, a pleasure seeker, who tried to forget everything through fun. And he was not a religionist who found the musings of the human spirit to be a quiet tranquilizer. On the contrary he was a Christian believer who saw in Jesus Christ, who died, yes, who was raised again, a reversal of every contradiction of life.

The Gospel is not only the message that in the death and resurrection of Christ we have eternal life. It is also the good news that Christ has overcome all the evil powers in this world, that He is with us in the midst of our struggles. In all things God makes us more than conquerors because in all things by the victory of Jesus Christ He reveals His suffering love and saving power. By the Lord's victory we have reason and hope to go on and go through, able to face anything without being beaten.

This Word is not only about some victory in the future, when the troubles of life are behind us. God holds out to us a victory now, one that we know in the midst of life's troubles. God has done more than simply wave a wand over us and suddenly everything is radiance and bliss. He had to do more than simply pronounce this huge reversal of His, this infinite rebuttal by which we have life instead of death, righteousness instead of condemnation, victory instead of defeat. He did it by going through it Himself, and having done it, He gives it to us right now.

The invasion of Normandy in World War II was an impressive military victory. That particular invasion was not a last-ditch effort on the part of the Allies to avoid defeat. It was planned rather as a clinching operation. You can imagine the great expectancy that swept through the troops as they hit the beaches. They could look back on the blood and sweat and tears with the smell of victory in their nostrils. They were more than conquerors!

We can also look back like that, with the cross and resurrection of Christ behind us, our hearts pounding with joy, because no matter how things may appear and no matter how real our troubles are, this is no time to feel defeated. God has moved in and made us more than conquerors.

With defeat behind us and victory within us it's time to live!

* 7

* 7

WHEN WE DON'T KNOW
WHICH END IS UP

Establishing the right priorities in life is very difficult. And our distorted sense of values haunts us. For instance, we practically mortgage away our lives just to purchase a new home, but in the background lurks a nagging concern about the homeless in the world. We perform a thousand little rituals. We engage in recreation, travel, spending sprees, social convention. We train our sights on goals: a good education, a good job, a happy home, a comfortable retirement. Yet we question the point of it all.

Very simply, we find it quite hard to get to the basics. Who wants to be bothered about ultimate questions when we live from day to day in a dog-eat-dog world? Who wants to give serious thought to world problems? Who even wants to take a good look at his marital or family or personal problems? It seems so much easier to repress everything. We would prefer to play every hypocritical game in the book in order to survive.

We tell ourselves that after all there is only one priority in life, and that is to be happy. We are convinced there is something or someone out in life who will give and guarantee what we think we've got coming. But it keeps escaping us. Our problems aren't solved just because we get married. That unexpected bonus provided only a temporary joy. Thirty years with the company, and all a person gets is a gold watch!

The priorities we put on life get turned upside down. We need Someone to set our lives right side up. Jesus Christ came to overcome our upside-down lives and to turn them right side up again. Our wrong values built on sin and disobedience He took to the cross. He rose from death as the Victor over all evil. He comes to us now to reverse the evil and renew the good. We look for some hope for the future, some way out of present predicaments. World problems, national problems, personal problems beg for answers.

In Jesus' day there were many who gravitated toward Him, intrigued by His words, fascinated by His miracles of healing. In Him they saw the promise of a better life.

But Jesus was not one to have people stumble after Him blindly or irrationally. He had a way of turning everything in life upside down.

Observe His method: "As they were going along the road, a man said to Him, 'I will follow You wherever You go.' And Jesus said to him, 'Foxes have holes, and the birds of the air have nests; but the Son of Man has nowhere to lay His head'" (Luke 9:57-58). Well, that's enough to make a man stop and scratch his head. Our

Lord warns us that He is a homeless man, and He seems to promise more insecurity instead of less.

Christ finds us worrying about what we are going to eat and drink and wear and wanting a place of our own. He beholds our illusions. His call raises a large question mark over our lives. Do we know which end is up? Do we see things right side up?

But our Lord is more than an exposer. He is also the revealer. He is there as the One who gives hope. He bids us follow Him through crucifixion and stand with Him in the reality of His resurrection and live with the One who owns all things. Now there is a priority that upsets all our priorities and still stands us on our feet.

Clearly He wants us to live with an earnest seriousness. "To another He said, 'Follow Me.' But he said, 'Lord, let me first go and bury my father.' But He said to him, 'Leave the dead to bury their own dead; but as for you, go and proclaim the kingdom of God.'" (9:59-60)

Now that's a hard saying. He is using a situation at hand to make very clear that there's no time to stop for the dead when Life itself is knocking at the door. And Jesus is saying that a man cannot give priority to any kind of law — even laws pertaining to the burial of the dead — when the new world of grace has broken into the world.

That hits us where it hurts. Following Christ takes precedence over obeying laws. We delude ourselves into thinking that our obedience of the commandments will give us security and identity. And Jesus says that is the way of death. In place of the frustration and futility that comes by the Law, Jesus instead promises the fulfillment of all law, the forgiveness of all sin. What He says upsets all our vain efforts and uncovers our death, but at the same time His Word is the gift of life. In discipleship with Him we walk and live.

We are caught up now in a life-and-death matter. "Another said, 'I will follow You, Lord; but let me first say farewell to those at my home.' Jesus said to him, 'No one who puts his hand to the plow and looks back is fit for the kingdom of God'" (9:61-62). His Word means there is to be no running back to what we were and who we were before He called us. The past is dead, over-come. A new beginning has taken place in us. We need never look back, because by His cross there is eternal life to live.

God has put some kind of new priority on us. We, the upside down, have been turned right side up.

When we don't know what end is up, Christ comes to us and says, "Follow Me." And then we know it's time to live.

* *8*

* *8*

WHEN THE STRENGTH ISN'T THERE

It takes strength to celebrate life. To celebrate is to say yes to the morning when it arrives. To celebrate is to say yes to life when you're growing old, when you're going home from the funeral of a loved one. To celebrate is to say yes to life when the world seems to be coming down around your ears.

The prophet Isaiah told his people: "Strengthen the weak hands, and make firm the feeble knees. Say to those who are of a fearful heart, 'Be strong, fear not!'" (Isaiah 35:3). At first his words must have sounded like a mockery. The people of Israel were in trouble as they usually were, whether with God or with some other nation. And when you are always slugging it out with someone else, no matter who it is, you don't get stronger. You become tired, feeble in the knees and fearful in the heart.

Israel was a weary nation, decadent because of incompetent leadership, disastrous foreign alliances, a corrupt priesthood, social injustices. Northern and southern kingdoms both finally collapsed. Captivity to an enemy power became the lot of the people. And all the prophet can seem to do is to cry, "Be strong."

Feeble knees and fearful hearts don't respond energetically to such urgings. Imagine the response of apathetic dropouts in our big cities if we encourage them to be strong. Say, "Be strong," to a weary black man in the ghetto, to a confused soldier on the battlefield, a worn-out housewife or businessman, a frightened child. When we suffer from disillusionment or despair, when we are fatigued physically and emotionally, when we are worn down with hostility and anxiety, we don't want to hear someone say, "Be strong." But the prophet doesn't seem to catch on. He not only says, "Be strong." He also adds, "Fear not!" As in Old Testament times, weariness, fatigue, and fear are part of life today. If we don't have the strength to stand on our feet and swing, we can't celebrate.

Israel lost heart. They were the chosen race, but experience seemed to contradict. They seemed to end up behind and under the Assyrians, the Persians, or the Egyptians. A beaten people doesn't have much heart left. Any words about not fearing are almost absurd.

Loss of heart is a common sickness today. We hear others say, "I have so much to be thankful for. I have everything I want. But I'm unhappy and afraid." Deprived of nothing, yet we are depressed. We're afraid of being cheated or exploited. We dread losing what we have — our status, our name, our family, our money, our rights. We are afraid of the conflict between black power and white power. We are afraid to give, afraid to love, afraid to live. Where is the strength to celebrate?

Surely not in ourselves, though we have strengths of our own — spirit, drive, stamina, energy, will, ambition. Yet what do we accomplish by our own strength? Sickness, failure, death, problems in our nation, our world, our cities, our churches. Feeble knees and fearful hearts are the result of living by our own strength. And we were never made for that.

We were made to live by God's strength. Nobody knew that better than the authors of the psalms. They speak for us:

> I am poured out like water, and all my bones are out of joint. My heart is like wax; it is melted in the midst of my bowels. My strength is dried like a potsherd. (22:14-15)

> I am counted with them that go down into the pit; I am as a man that hath no strength. (88:4)

But they don't stop there:

> I called upon the Lord in distress; the Lord answered me and set me in a large place. The Lord is on my side; I will not fear. What can man do unto me? . . . It is better to trust in the Lord than to put confidence in man. . . . The

Lord is my Strength and Song and is become my Salvation. (118:5-6, 8, 14)

God is our Refuge and Strength, a very present Help in trouble. Therefore will not we fear though the earth be removed and though the mountains be carried into the midst of the sea, though the waters thereof roar and be troubled, though the mountains shake with the swelling thereof. (46:1-3)

When the prophet Isaiah says, "Be strong," and, "Fear not," we can be sure he is not appealing to anything within ourselves. He is not trying to make us believe that we can go on if we just try harder.

He directs his people away from themselves and says, "Behold, your God . . . will come and save you" (Isaiah 35:4). He tells them that "the eyes of the blind shall be opened and the ears of the deaf unstopped. Then shall the lame man leap like a hart and the tongue of the dumb sing for joy" (35:5). He says all this to a people that no longer has a leg to stand on, that is broken-hearted and despairing. But he gives them a reason to go on. He gives them hope by giving them the promise and Word of God. He holds before them the strength of God.

If we think for a moment that God is not up to what He says, that He cannot deliver us, it is time to take another look at what He does. Not only did the Old Testament people return from exile, but God had a larger rescue in mind. When John the Baptist was in prison, trembling with feeble knees and a fearful heart, he sent word to Jesus with the question: "Are You He who is to come, or shall we look for another?" And Jesus' answer: "Go and tell John what you hear and see: the blind receive their sight and the lame walk, lepers are cleansed and the deaf hear, and the dead are raised up, and the poor have good news preached to them." (Matthew 11:4-5)

God did it all in Jesus Christ. Our Lord bared God's strength. Though drained of all strength on the cross, He offered Himself to God in death. That was a saving act, a healing Word. And now risen in victory, He lives as the Strong One with help and hope for His people.

He gives strength to celebrate, to stand up and take heart, to return to life. We can look at world conditions for what they are, knowing that God is still in charge. He gives strength to celebrate our marriage, our daily calling, our mortal existence. He gives strength to feeble knees and fearful hearts.

The writer to the Hebrews put it this way:

Therefore lift your drooping hands and strengthen your weak knees, and make straight paths for your feet, so that what is lame may not be put out of joint but rather be healed. Strive for peace with all men and for the holiness without which no one will see the Lord. See to it that no one fail to obtain the grace of God, that no "root of bitterness" spring up and cause trouble and by it the many become defiled. . . . Therefore let us be grateful for receiving a kingdom that cannot be shaken, and thus let us offer to God acceptable worship with reverence and awe. (Hebrews 12:12-15, 28)

When our strength isn't there, God can create a time to live.